SHOSTAKOVICH

Oxford Studies of Composers
General Editor : Colin Mason

Egon Wellesz: FUX
Denis Arnold: MARENZIO
Basil Deane: CHERUBINI
Paul Doe: TALLIS
Anthony Payne: SCHOENBERG
Ian Kemp: HINDEMITH
Jerome Roche: PALESTRINA
Gilbert Reaney: MACHAUT

Oxford Studies of Composers (8)

SHOSTAKOVICH

NORMAN KAY

London

OXFORD UNIVERSITY PRESS

Oxford University Press, Ely House, London W.1

GLASGOW   NEW YORK   TORONTO   MELBOURNE   WELLINGTON
CAPE TOWN   IBADAN   NAIROBI   DAR ES SALAAM   LUSAKA   ADDIS ABABA
DELHI   BOMBAY   CALCUTTA   MADRAS   KARACHI   LAHORE   DACCA
KUALA LUMPUR   SINGAPORE   HONG KONG   TOKYO

ISBN 0 19 315422 6

First Published 1971
Second Impression 1972

The music examples in this book are reproduced by permission
of Anglo–Soviet Music Press Ltd. with the exception of
Ex. 7 which is published by Universal Edition.

Printed in Great Britain
by W & J Mackay Limited, Chatham

CONTENTS

INTRODUCTION

Prolific, traditional, functional almost in the eighteenth-century sense of the word, Shostakovich is an important composer, representing an essential aspect of conservatism in twentieth-century music, a gradual expansion from the secure base of a widely-accepted tradition. It is an attitude which appears anachronistic to many Western musicians, but which nevertheless may provide a foundation for future development. That it should be the leading composer of a so-called radical society who plays such a conservative role is an interesting phenomenon. But art has very often counterbalanced the trends visible in the outside world, and Shostakovich's conservatism is, in reality, no more surprising than the radicalism of Mussorgsky when seen against that composer's static social background.

The aim of this short study is obviously not a comprehensive survey of the whole of Shostakovich's vast output. Instead, a number of key works, not necessarily from a purely stylistic point of view, but also from the point of view of their impact on the composer's artistic environment, have been chosen for discussion. Thus, the Fifth Symphony is given a good deal of space, even though it is possible to argue that the Second or Eighth symphonies deserve equal emphasis. In a similar way, *Katerina Ismailova*, the String Quartet No. 8, and the Symphony No. 10 are discussed as much for their external impact as for their intrinsic qualities. The two aspects are in fact quite inseparable in the case of Shostakovich. There seems little point in isolating the minutiae of style, if outside pressures are ignored. Equally, a review of Soviet politico-artistic aims alone cannot provide a clue to the composer's real outlook and achievement. No single work can begin to show his importance and no neat political theory can be applied to him. Between these extremes lies the reality, discoverable only if we refuse to surrender either to political slogans or to a worship of internal musical formulae. Only then can a relevant picture of Shostakovich emerge: a man often subjected to immense pressure, yet, in spite of this, an artist able to maintain a consistent viewpoint in his music.

Undoubtedly at certain times a tension has been felt between his personal introversion and the need for external social optimism. But this tension, while leading to a number of caricatures, notably in some of the 'positive' symphonic finales, has also helped to sustain the vitality underlying what might otherwise appear to be merely a diffuse, outdated language. Time and again, Shostakovich's work is saved from banality or dullness by a spark which leaps across the gap between the intrinsic nature of his thought and its final expression. His external needs sometimes force him to choose a wide symphonic space for his ideas, even if their real nature is more pithy or laconic than might be expected from their context. Similarly, he preserves tonality as a communications bridge to the outside world, even when the linear or harmonic needs of a passage seem to cut across any explicit tonal foundation. Both spatially and vertically, tension can build up between the nature of his work and its ultimate form. In Western criticism, this pull of opposing tendencies has usually been regarded as a weakness, and enthusiasm has been reserved for the works in which either the tension is at its lowest—the private world of the string quartets, for example—or has itself become the subject for overt drama, as in the tension between the internal (solo) and external (orchestral) worlds of the string concertos. These works are indeed important, but in the long run, the case for Shostakovich rests on wider achievements: first, that during a period when the survival of the symphony in Russia was at stake, he managed to justify its artistic validity by a gargantuan effort of will centred on the Fifth Symphony; second, that throughout his career, a consistent view of expanded tonality and its disciplines has been in evidence. The works that form the basis for this study are those in which these related facts are most clearly shown.

EARLY WORKS

The works written during Shostakovich's student period at the Leningrad Conservatoire are dominated by the piano. His Three Fantastic Dances were intended for performance by himself, and they certainly show an intimate knowledge of the instrument's possibilities. But beyond this, they also display features which recur in his early orchestral works. They are based on single ideas, juxtaposed to provide linear continuity. The themes themselves are spiky, the harmonies ambiguous in the manner of Prokofiev, whose piano works and 'Classical' Symphony were part of the staple musical diet in Leningrad. Behind this obvious influence, another more pervasive one was apparent—that of Schumann. The struggle to compress lyrical ideas into a small musical area is derived from that composer, as is the attempt to introduce ideas derived from the theatre.

These facts are important when we look at the work with which Shostakovich first made a wide general impact—the First Symphony, written in 1926 when he was nineteen. Undoubtedly, Prokofiev's 'Classical' Symphony was a strong influence, as was Stravinsky's *Petrushka*. The flavour of both works can be felt in the symphony, and there is a fairly direct reference to the 'Valse' from the Stravinsky work in the flute theme of the first movement (Ex. 1). But a more noticeable

Ex. 1

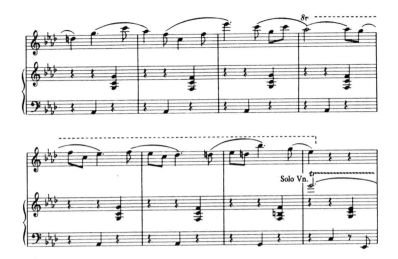

influence, and one which continued into more mature works, was that of the Russian theatre. This was the era of the new mass theatre supervised by Meyerhold, and it is understandable that a young composer would feel its magnetic attraction. From the very first trumpet and bassoon notes of the symphony's introduction, we are in a world that is theatrical in the *commedia dell'arte* sense of the word. And this image is maintained throughout the movement.

The opening section is interesting in a number of ways. Only once does its harmony settle on a tonal centre—and then on the largely irrelevant one of A major. The initial phrase has an inbuilt ambiguity which causes the fifty-seven bars of introduction to twist and turn from one tonal hint to another (Ex. 2). By refusing to form a complete statement, this phrase impels the action forward—an impression heightened by the

Ex. 2

large number of gaps in the structure. These theatrical breaks also emphasize the preparatory nature of the material, as if the young composer were probing for a suitable thematic basis for the movement.

Characteristically, when Shostakovich does arrive at a sufficiently firm theme, his tonality settles down to its first sustained key—F minor. He commits himself to this tonal centre by repeating the outline of the ironic march theme which it supports no less than four times, before passing on to an expanded use of the material (Ex. 3). But the line is interrupted

Ex. 3

by a phrase from the introduction, heralding, again in theatrical manner, the more relaxed waltz theme. This second subject belies its metrical layout. Without the help of the score, one would assume for a number of bars that the accentuation of the theme and its accompaniment occurred on the first beat of the bar. And indeed there seems little reason why it should not have done, since its link to the next full-bar phrase is not particularly notable, differing in this respect from the models on which the device was obviously based, in Schumann and Brahms. Neither of those masters would have allowed any final uncertainty in the listener's mind as to the exact position of the main beat: their whole idea was to produce a shock when the music reverted to its true metrical shape.

The rest of the movement consists of a dialogue between the march and the waltz; but for most of the time, this dialogue is purely one of linear juxtaposition. In other words, the two elements are treated as separate aspects of a continuous narration, rather than as a pair of complementary units which can be drawn into symphonic unity. True, there is a moment in the development when it appears that Shostakovich is about to explore the possibilities of their integration (Ex. 4). Here is the

Ex. 4

opportunity for a real meeting-point. But the implications are not followed through in the way that a more contrapuntally gifted composer might have achieved. Instead, the waltz structure becomes a mere decoration after a very short time. Nevertheless the seeds are sown here for a number of Shostakovich's later symphonic developments—the opening movement of the Tenth Symphony comes to mind immediately. And the way in which the movement sinks to rest at the point from which it started out is also prophetic of a large number of subsequent symphonic structures.

One of the most outstanding features of the whole piece is its economy of texture. There are very few passages in which the orchestra is fully deployed, and even then the part-writing remains clear throughout. This is in such marked contrast to the scoring of similar passages in the middle symphonies that it raises a number of interesting points. Over-scoring, as Vaughan Williams was honest enough to admit, is usually a sign of lack of confidence in the basic quality of the musical material. If this is true of Shostakovich, the external crisis of 1936—the condemnation of *Lady Macbeth of Mtsensk*—was already mirrored and anticipated in the thought processes of the Third and Fourth Symphonies, where subject matter no more significant than the opening movement of the First Symphony was grossly inflated and elongated. But at the age of nineteen, there was no apparent self-doubt: the narrative method employed, the concise exposition of themes, the economy of texture, all point to a remarkable honesty and confidence, not to mention mastery of orchestral style.

The opening movement is the outstanding achievement of the symphony; the rest is much less significant, though displaying in embryonic form features which grow in importance through later works. The scherzo-like second movement borrows its outline from the finale of Prokofiev's 'Classical' Symphony, even down to the runs that punctuate the texture in both works. The slow movement, on the other hand, reveals a great deal about Shostakovich's private world. It is filled with nostalgia, conveyed as much by shifting harmonies as by the shape of the main melody itself. In his spontaneous innocence, the young composer gives this mood its full rein— something which his later self-criticism, reinforced by official disapproval, would rarely allow. In some of the more mature works, this kind of introverted lyricism—'neurasthenia' was Zhdanov's hysterical description during one of the Party diatribes—would be transmuted and generalized, usually by the use of more 'objective' folk-songs, or the celebration of collective national tragedies. But here it stands as a fully individual, clearly stated emotion. The last movement, in a way, is similarly prophetic, in the sense that its implications resound through a number of his later orchestral finales. Its attempt to solve what might be called the European finale-problem is far from successful. Part of its failure undoubtedly stems from the fact that the main theme simply does not have the stamina or the character to sustain a movement of this size; it is little more than a phrase, with the result that Shostakovich searches endlessly around it and away from it in the hope of enlarging its scope (Ex. 5). Like so many of the 'optimistic' finales of subsequent symphonies, this one sounds forced and hollow. The main problem is one of function—the physical energy displayed is vastly in excess of the real nature of the material.

The works immediately following the First Symphony continued to pursue a reasonably exploratory course. The Prelude and Scherzo for strings—labelled Op. 11, though most of it was completed before the symphony—looks forward in style to the declamatory opening of the Piano Quintet, written in 1940. The atmosphere in the new Soviet state was at this time still

Ex. 5

surprisingly liberal, and numerous Western composers—Hindemith, Krenek, and Berg, for instance—were freely performed and discussed. In politics, also, a certain measure of freedom was initiated by Lenin in the New Economic Policy (1921–7), with the resumption of private ownership on a limited scale. Theatres featured Western avant-garde drama, the art galleries exhibited Picasso and the works of other leading cubists. Even jazz appeared on the musical scene, becoming in fact something of a popular craze. Against this background, Shostakovich's early style was far from revolutionary. His innate conservatism was apparent even in works which were, on the surface, unusually enterprising. Thus, in his First Piano Sonata, again dating from that extraordinary year, 1926, he tries out freely dissonant textures, but then abruptly retreats into unison or triadic writing (Ex. 6). Even more characteristic of this period were his Ten Aphorisms for piano, a set

Ex. 6

of short pieces, spiky yet inconsistent in their modernity. Largely confined to two-part textures, they were later condemned by their composer in a revealing way: 'I was pursuing abstract experimentation—the pieces were an erroneous striving after originality.'

In the opera *The Nose*, based on Gogol's story, Shostakovich is again seen straining at the leash of musical convention. A short example from the overture will show how far he travelled stylistically in the three years between the composition of the First Symphony and this work. Here, no attempt is made to provide tonal roots for the proliferating satire; nor is there any attempt to look closely at the nature of the emerging chromaticism. Textures are sparse, but the overriding impression is of an indeterminate and ambiguous line, on the move the whole time, though to no really clear artistic purpose (Ex. 7).

According to Shostakovich, the opera was 'written in merriment'; it was a satire aimed at most of the accepted canons of opera. In fact, its overall form tilts not only at standard opera, but also at the conventions of theatre itself. The basic story

18

recounts the tale of Major Kovalev's nose, lost by its hapless owner, searched for in the course of the work, and finally restored. But at the end of the ninth scene, which is called 'Epilogue' by the composer, there recurs the conversation between Kovalev and his barber with which the opera began. As if to undermine the whole sense of sequential time, this epilogue is by no means the end of the work; Shostakovich continues into a tenth scene, again a conversation-piece featuring Kovalev. Soviet commentators, wise after the event, later declared that the entire opera was an attempt to score at the expense of the audience—an elaborate hoax, and the first signs of a dangerous gulf between composer and public. True or false, the opera certainly confirmed Shostakovich's new role as the *enfant terrible* of Russian music.

With the beginning of Stalin's rule, the political climate gradually changed. His first Five Year Plan (1928) envisaged a gigantic expansion of Russian industry, the collectivization of the farms, and the elimination of the kulaks or rich peasants. Parallel with this, a campaign was initiated to cut out all signs of Western 'degeneracy' in art. Contemporary European music was virtually banned; no jazz was allowed to filter through the new boundary. Almost the only styles to find official favour were the routine marches, songs, and dances written by members of the Association of Proletarian Musicians—and in 1929 these proletarian groups reigned supreme over Russian music. The official edicts began to show unintended hilarity in their dogmatic and sweeping appraisals, one of their outstanding efforts being the denigration of Tchaikovsky as a deplorable bourgeois deviation, a lacuna in Russian history. But the Proletarian art movements were inept even as entertainment, and they were dissolved in 1932, though not before they had produced a marked effect on a number of notable composers, including Shostakovich. These outside pressures were, in fact, of crucial importance to the developing young composer; they forced him to become increasingly self-conscious, and they undermined his musical confidence. More vulnerable than many composers because of his work in the more public media of theatre and cinema—by 1933, he had written the music for five films and six plays—Shostakovich suffered increasingly from a kind of split focus in his output. On the one hand, the symphonies up to No. 4 continued the stylistic trends of the earlier works, though progressively adding to the density and inflation of resources. On the other hand, a group of much smaller works contradicted this tendency by concentrating on linear writing, cool neo-classical forms, and succinct under-statement. It was as if the composer, driven in one direction by his effort to meet public pressure, was compensating by preserving an aloof, meditative inner world, untainted by any external maelstrom.

Outstanding among the group of 'interior' works produced at this time were the Twenty-Four Preludes, written in 1932–3. Their deliberately simplified style points forward, not only to the much later Preludes and Fugues, but to the outlook implicit in the private works which were to become a crucial factor in bringing him through the difficult years ahead. Almost all his subsequent chamber music grew from the seeds planted in this one work. The first of the preludes sets the flavour of the whole group. It is basically diatonic, and its rhythmic and harmonic structure is regular. Against this determined simplicity, one or two moments of harmonic ambiguity are allowed to add their piquant effect (Ex. 8), but they are never in a position to disturb the even flow of the music. The fourth Prelude, in E minor, shows the composer's increasing interest in fugal writing, with its series of entries on various degrees of the scale. The fact that this particular prelude is cast in $\frac{5}{4}$ time, with its oblique stresses, brings it into line with some of the piano writing of Hindemith, an interesting comparison when we think of the later Preludes and Fugues

Ex. 8

in relation to Hindemith's *Ludus Tonalis*. The attraction of fugue form for Shostakovich reflected not only his admiration for the keyboard works of Bach, but also his determination, throughout his piano works, not to be seduced by the instrument's capacity for surface effect—mere percussiveness, or, at the other extreme, mere woolly atmosphere. Clearly, he felt that this most autocratic of instruments must be disciplined and regulated by being forced to submit to the strictest of all forms. In a way, this austerity served as atonement for the increasing prolixity of the orchestral works. No better example of this renunciation can be given than the fourth Prelude—from many points of view the most important of the whole group. Its structure is tightly controlled, but even more important, its polyphonic movement sets up an oblique kind of pantonality which becomes more relaxed and expansive as more voices are added. Yet it is only at the climactic bar, a mere eight bars from the end, that it is necessary for Shostakovich to step outside the range of diatonic intervals which has formed the entire language of the movement. Up to that point, his tensions and resolutions have been achieved solely by the cross-currents produced between the simplest of intervals and lines.

It would be foolish to claim originality for this type of composition in 1933. Stravinsky's linear, Bach-inspired works—

the Piano Sonata and the Concerto for piano and wind instruments among others—had preceded the Shostakovich Preludes by several years. And Hindemith was already fashioning a theoretical basis which would embrace not only such linear writing, but also a much more chromatic, radical conflation of parts. It is safe to say, however, that no other Soviet composer of that time was pursuing such formal discipline—Prokofiev, the one exception, retained in some ways the outlook of a mid-European composer, and cannot therefore be included within the limits of Soviet music.

On the other side of the composer's output were the large-scale works culminating in the Fourth Symphony, which represents a kind of zenith of size and duration. The orchestra employed is mammoth—quadruple woodwind, eight trumpets, two tubas and a sizeable battery of percussion instruments. Only a few bars from the beginning, Shostakovich is using the full array in massive chords and furious unison outbursts. There is no reticence here, no attempt to mould the orchestral size to the needs of the musical material. For it must be admitted that the ideas contained in the first movement do not of themselves require anything like the resources that are heaped on them in such abandoned profusion. The main theme, for instance, first heard on the violins, is spiky, with a touch of the grotesque in the increasing size of the intervals used. Yet it is thrust outward with an unremitting show of heavy power (Ex. 9). Even more grotesque is the presto fugato

Ex. 9

section of this opening movement; one string part is added to another until a dense, rushing body of sound is finally punctuated by woodwind and brass. The general impression is of unwarranted size and flatulence; the intrinsic musical qualities are very questionable. The obvious intention is to overwhelm the listener by force, so it is no surprise when the finale of the symphony, after progressing from largo to march to vast waltz—a gigantic parody of the opening movement of the First Symphony—culminates in a desperate gallop, and comes to a sprawling end in one of the longest pedal C codas ever dreamed up by a European composer. It is difficult to see how Shostakovich could have travelled much further along the road that his 'public' works were taking, and the Fourth Symphony was in some ways a point of no return. He was never again to attempt a structure of such staggering complexity. But in fact the work did not reach the stage of a public performance. Shostakovich withdrew it during rehearsal, perhaps because he had become aware of the uproar its performance might have caused. He has since stated that his sole reason for withdrawal was his own dissatisfaction with the finale. Whatever the reason, the symphony disappeared from sight, to be rescued and given performance only in the 1960s. Within days of its withdrawal, a government decree was issued, condemning formalism and individualism in music, and singling out for particular opprobrium Shostakovich's opera *Lady Macbeth of Mtsensk* (since renamed *Katerina Ismailova*).

CRISIS

At first sight, this 1936 decree appears very much like a number of earlier instructions from the Party, except perhaps for the virulence of its language. Few previous decrees had used terms such as 'neuropathic discords', 'grinding, squealing roars', or 'muddle instead of music', but the general idea of regulating and closely supervising not only the aims but also the methods of Soviet artists was of course nothing new. In 1934, the date of *Lady Macbeth*'s first performance, the concept of socialist realism had been formulated by Gorky at the first convention of the Soviet Literary Union and applied to all media by an increasing flow of articles, minor decrees, or peremptory injunctions. There was, as usual, no shortage of mentors to help in its interpretation. And yet, the singling out of *Lady Macbeth* for such excoriation remains one of the mysteries of Soviet music. Its first appearance had been a great success, and it had been playing to packed houses ever since. The most intelligent and influential critic on the scene, Boris Asafiev, had written: 'The character of Katerina is drawn with great sympathy—it adds a valuable quality to Shostakovich's music, of warmth, femininity, and tenderness.' And, both at home and abroad, the opera seemed to fulfil every requirement from an ideological point of view: it threw a spotlight on the corruption which Marxism would think inevitable in an idle, over-rich bourgeois household, as well as making clear that its unsympathetic characters were in fact pawns, imprisoned by their circumstances just as much as any of their victims. In musical style, too, it fulfilled most of the explicit requirements of Soviet music, very rarely losing sight of a tonal centre, and then only for immediate visual or dramatic effect, as in the interlude before the murder of Katerina's father-in-law. It was, in short, hailed as a model of the new Soviet art when it first appeared—an ideal to be studied and imitated by other composers. In view of this, it seems incredible that, within two years, such an official volte-face could have taken place, especially if one remembers that a number of more disruptive works written about the same time—*The Dipsomaniac* by Marian Koval was perhaps the most notable—were allowed to survive.

The real background to the crisis may never come to light. There were signs that the decree followed a visit to the opera by Stalin himself, and that he was responsible for the exact wording of the attack. Yet, on the evidence of his daughter Svetlana, Stalin was an inveterate theatre-goer. It seems unlikely that this important example of socialist realism could have escaped his attention for two years, during which it had captured the headlines and become, in a sense, a piece of Soviet history. But these two years had also seen a rapid deterioration in political affairs. Stalin's second Five Year Plan, introduced in 1933, again concentrated on a massive industrial effort, with the inevitable prospect of yet another period of intense hardship. Contacts with the outside world were discouraged, partly no doubt to prevent depressing news from leaking out, and partly to prevent the 'contamination' of Soviet art by more liberal Western attitudes. And, while the facts were desperate, Soviet artists must nevertheless produce images of a rosy existence. 'Life is Better, Life is Happier' was the slogan they were forced to adopt; and the characteristic poster-coloured picture of Soviet youth appeared, thrusting forward into a glowing future, with arms raised in triumph. Nothing could be allowed to contradict this blinkered, pseudo-optimistic image.

Perhaps one need look no further for the reason behind the attack on *Lady Macbeth*. Starkly negative in subject, it presented an easy target, as well as being the most significant opera yet produced in the Soviet state. If so, the timing of the decree remains a mystery, as does the hysteria of its language. I believe there was more to this particular conflict than was made explicit in the decree, and the clue is given not only in the Asafiev review quoted earlier, but also in the words of Shostakovich himself. The opera was intended to form the first part of a tetralogy dealing with Russian woman in a number of historical and social situations—a series of portraits linked by their celebration of a feminine image. For this purpose, the original Leskov story, on which the opera was based, presented obvious difficulties. For Leskov, Katerina was a squalid, selfish criminal—hemmed in by a hostile, boring environment, perhaps, but deserving the condemnation which she encountered. Shostakovich softens this portrait by a number of means. Thus, the hostile world is emphasized by a hardening of the character of Katerina's father-in-law, Boris, for whom Shostakovich composed some of his most malevolent music. And, when Katerina is attracted, largely out of boredom, to one of her husband's employees, Sergei, the latter is pictured as entirely unworthy of her—as brutal as her husband is weak and ineffective. Two crimes are committed—the murder of Boris by Katerina, and that of her husband by Sergei—but Shostakovich, as he later said, intended his music to minimize her own guilt. 'The musical language of the whole opera is intended to exonerate Katerina' he declared, and, in the fourth act of the opera, when retribution has overtaken both herself and Sergei, this is precisely the effect it has; her music becomes increasingly warm and sympathetic, until it culminates in a moving monologue, just before her suicide. When all is understood, all is forgiven, the music insists.

This is, I suggest, the core of the dispute. At a time when the survival of the state was felt to be in danger, and a huge, essentially masculine effort was demanded, the attitude of tender understanding, feminine-inspired, was anathema to the authorities. Inadvertently, this work threatened to undermine and to compromise the hard, forward-looking determination of its audiences; it was therefore an object for unique wrath. Of course, any discussion of official motives must be speculative in the circumstances. But this does offer an explanation of the otherwise strange fact that the decree was directed against a work less dissonant than, for instance, *The Nose*, less complex than the Second or Third Symphonies, and less disruptively satirical than Koval's two operas.

The external effect of the attack was obvious and serious enough. But it also brought to a head the internal crisis of style which had been building up around Shostakovich's public works. Indeed, the composer's treatment of the *Lady Macbeth* subject reveals a good deal about his inner world. From the start of his career, Shostakovich was a lyricist; his forms tended to spring from line rather than from tightly controlled structure. True, his theatrical, dramatic instinct heightened his sense of contrast, but the element of opposition—the sonata principal—was still subordinate to the overall atmosphere of a continuously linked form, occupying various levels of expressive intensity at different points of a movement. It is a notoriously difficult image to mould into a satisfactory symphonic shape, but the instinctive method seems to be cyclical, using that word in the mathematical sense of a line returning into itself to form a closed curve. Thus, many of Shostakovich's finest movements finish at the point at which they began; they return to their original source. In Jungian terms, it is an enclosed, anima-inspired image, which does not always find a satisfactory outlet in the more open-ended conflict of dualities in sonata form. (This touches on a large subject which is outside the scope of this study, but which offers a more precise analogy for the relationship between image and form in composers as widely separated in time as Schubert, Schumann,

Mahler, Berg, and Shostakovich himself—a relationship for which the label 'romantic' has often had to suffice.)

Certainly, *Lady Macbeth* shows the composer's instinctive bias very clearly. Inspired no doubt by the unity of image and form which was so outstanding a feature of Berg's *Wozzeck*, Shostakovich similarly adopted the device of using integral interludes and passacaglia-based forms, rather than separate arias and choruses. This continuously evolving orchestral line was more than usually necessary because Shostakovich used a libretto which had its roots, not in formal verse, but in natural, relatively unshaped conversation. The method was not entirely consistent, however, and there are a number of sections which are uneven since neither verbal outline nor musical form was sufficiently significant. Thus, the meandering woodwind lines of the first scene may express Katerina's boredom but fail to impose themselves on a voice part which only gradually begins to take on its own outline. A little later, the music for the section in which Katerina is forced to swear her faithfulness before an icon is illustrative rather than musically important. But when verbal naturalism fuses with a significant musical form, as in the two scenes—the flogging of Sergei and the poisoning of Boris—which are linked by an interlude based on a free passacaglia, the result is some of the most impressive and dramatic music which Shostakovich had yet written.

In general, although flawed in places, the opera represented a break-through which could have had immense importance for Russian music. It was a genuine development of the naturalism in works such as Mussorgsky's *Boris Godunov*, and could very well have provided a viable basis, not only for the three further operas which Shostakovich had planned on similar lines, but also for the works of younger Soviet composers. As it was, Shostakovich understandably abandoned opera, leaving unfinished his only subsequent essay, *The Gamblers*, a satire based on Gogol's story. Wisely perhaps, he preferred to avoid a medium in which the normally intangible issues of instrumental music are literally given flesh, made explicit and tangible, and therefore more vulnerable to official interference. Instead, he was obliged to work out the problems of style in an abstract medium—the symphony. The measure of his success was that in emerging from this trauma, he managed not only to rehabilitate himself, but also to restore the symphony as a tolerated art form under the Soviet regime.

RETURN

Naturally enough, there was, by Shostakovich's standards, a considerable gap before the Fifth Symphony, the work which re-established him. Between the crisis of January 1936 and the symphony's first performance in October 1937 he produced only the Four Romanzas, Op. 46 and a small amount of incidental music. From the internal evidence of the Fifth Symphony itself, it is not easy to understand the work's significance from the Soviet point of view. If formalism was the greatest of all artistic sins, as the Party declared, and abstract or individualist goals were to be eschewed, it seems paradoxical that this symphony was, to date, the most abstract—in the sense of its close ties with sonata form—of all his symphonic works. Again, if as the Party said there must be no hint of tragedy in Soviet art, the first movement of the symphony presented a problem, since it posed a dark drama that constantly bordered on the tragic. All art was supposed to reflect folk or national idioms in order to meet its new public on the broadest possible ground, yet there is scarcely a hint of either element in the symphony. In the face of these paradoxes, the official reception of this new work must have been at best unpredictable. And the fact that Shostakovich held firm to his symphonic aims shows a high degree of personal courage at a time when artistic aberrations were only too easily translated into political crimes.

From the point of view of the musical style, there were however a number of important changes of direction. The most obvious of these is in the matter of economy. The mammoth orchestra of the Fourth Symphony has disappeared. In

the place of quadruple woodwind and eight trumpets, the new
work uses a fairly normal orchestra, with the exception perhaps of the two harps. It also avoids any overcomplex treatment of themes; no single idea is inflated beyond its real
capacity. If the scale of utterance reverts to that of the First
Symphony, the clarity of style owes a great deal to the Twenty-
Four Preludes for piano. As far as this neo-classicism is concerned, it is worth noting the similarity between the themes of
the first movement and the thematic content of Stravinsky's
Apollon Musagète, which had made its appearance in 1928. It
may be pure coincidence, but the formal introduction, with its
insistence on dotted rhythms, is common to both, and the
second theme of Shostakovich's work bears a marked resem-
blance to one of Stravinsky's floating melodies over relatively
static accompaniments (Ex. 10). But Shostakovich's intention

Ex. 10

is more programmatic, and this is perhaps one of the main reasons why the work was finally acceptable to the Party. As he himself said, the purpose of the symphony was 'to show the making of a man. I saw man with all his experiences in the centre of the composition, which is lyrical in form from beginning to end. The finale is the optimistic solution of the tragically tense moments of the first movement.' Behind the composer's complete statement on the work there lies not only the anxiety to cover any anticipated official criticism, but also the attempt to defend the presence of tragedy in symphonic writing. And if the last movement consists largely of the routine optimism demanded by the Stalin edicts, it is nevertheless framed within a clear symphonic shape.

The greatest interest of the new symphony lies in the first movement, for it is here that Shostakovich concentrates most of his musical thought. A comparison with the opening movement of the First Symphony reveals many points of similarity in structure, as well as contrasts in thematic material. While in some ways regressing to his original formal mould, however, Shostakovich has produced a much more balanced movement; there is more continuity of material, and this is distributed over the whole time-span with more assurance and calculation. The movement opens with a peremptory, assertive phrase in close canon (Ex. 11). Its chromatic licence is more apparent than real, for although it ranges through a number of mutually contradictory pivots, its foundation is the semitonal drop from B♭ to A, and the subsequent phrase discloses that this has in fact been the dominant to the main key of the work, D minor.

Ex. 11

It is interesting to notice the cadential nature of these first four bars; their pull towards the A sounds remarkably final, and only the twist to the D centre makes continuity possible. This habit of contradicting an apparently fixed cadence was to become one of Shostakovich's regularly used methods of achieving two opposed aims—to define a tonality while expanding beyond its ordinary limits. And the placing of cadential material so early in a movement is also a feature of the later symphonies, where it is often used not only for punctuation and tonal definition, but as a way of adding expressive weight to some of the slow opening statements. This first phrase is interesting in other ways too. Its widest intervals occur at the beginning, so that after a bar and a half, the opening thrust is already contracting into relative immobility, thus reinforcing the impression of a premature cadence, and reinforcing also the impression that the next phrase, with its softer line and more stable accompaniment, forms the necessary answering half of the whole idea. This tension-resolution syndrome acts as a microcosm of the whole movement, and indeed, in a more programmatic sense, of the entire symphony, with its progression from the stresses of the first movement to the assurance of the finale.

One of the most noticeable signs of Shostakovich's development as a composer is the way in which he now manages to integrate the various links and accompaniment figures into the general texture. Almost invariably, these are closely derived from some aspect of the previous thematic material, so that there is a kind of overlapping effect—theme becoming accompaniment to the next theme—and consequently a continuity of invention which no longer depends entirely on pace or dynamic contrast. From a symphonic point of view, this is a significant advance on the technique of dramatic punctuation and sudden changes of gear that proliferated in the First Symphony; it leads to an internally generated stability, from which a real expansion of form becomes possible. Thus, as early as the transition between the first and second halves of the opening subject, the dotted rhythm of (a) becomes, with only slight modification, the rhythmic basis for (b) (Ex. 11), and there is an obvious attempt to carry forward the various elements which both parts contain. Similarly, when it comes to the second-subject complex, the repeated chords of the accompaniment provide the shape of the transition to the central development section (Ex. 12), and are themselves derived from a motif taken from the previous subject. Perhaps there is still too much material in this long exposition, but it is interlocked and organized in a way not found in any of Shostakovich's

Ex. 12

earlier symphonies. The second subject, with its wide yet diatonic intervals and its lack of incident—at least when compared with the first section—gives the impression of a deliberate effort to hold the music out at arm's length, so to speak; hence its similarity to *Apollon Musagète*, and to Shostakovich's own Fourth Prelude for piano. It relies entirely on single-line melody with the simplest of triadic accompaniments, and contains no hint of imitation, canonic or otherwise. There is no doubt that in reducing the surface tension of the music in this way, Shostakovich intended to symbolize his attempt to reach out beyond the confines of individual style. And it is significant that in the coda to the movement, the more active opening motif is gradually submerged beneath similarly static harmonies; it sinks under its own weight, becoming finally a mere supporting texture.

The three remaining movements of the symphony require less comment. They follow a fairly predictable pattern, without disturbing the proportions of the work as a whole. The obvious attempt of the last movement to be positive and optimistic continues to recur with painful regularity in the succeeding symphonic works, and, with its undertones of Slav hysteria, is no more convincing here than in the later examples. One important detail about this finale concerns its derivation. As noted, the only concert work to see the light of day during 1936 was the Four Romanzas, Op. 46. A phrase from these settings appears again in this finale, during the episode before the coda. The words, from Pushkin, are revealing: 'And the doubts pass away from my troubled soul, As a fresh, brighter day brings visions of pure gold.'

DICHOTOMY

With all his professional confidence restored by the tremendous success of the new work, Shostakovich was nevertheless unable to achieve the total integration of language that seemed to be the aim of the opening movement. Instead, he was obliged to pursue two different paths simultaneously, and if anything, to accentuate the very gap between personal and public image which the Fifth Symphony was intended to resolve. With only his music for the film *Volochayev Days* intervening, he launched himself into the series of chamber works by which his reputation was secured in the eyes of the outside world. The first work in this chain was the First String Quartet, composed in 1938: in it the real composer is to be found. This is not, of course, to say that the chamber works invariably carry a heavy burden of philosophy in the Beethovenian sense. The tradition of Russian writing, particularly for string quartet, is much more relaxed, and the intellectual content is not so inexorably concentrated. The First Quartet is a perfect example of this relaxed approach. It uses the medium with the ease of a well-loved, familiar suit of clothes, and produces a naïvely simple, immediate impression. The thematic material of the first movement, for instance, is almost derisively uncomplicated (Ex. 13). It is entirely monodic, and the idiom remains determinedly diatonic throughout. Equally important, from the point of view of Shostakovich's future as a chamber music composer, there is no attempt to expand the ideas beyond the natural limits imposed by four solo strings. This may be labouring the obvious point that a string quartet is, after all, different in

37

Ex. 13

Moderato

genre from a symphony, but it is of some significance in the case of a composer whose work is not particularly noted for its sparse use of the available resources. It argues a more conscious, deliberate self-discipline than might be expected.

This trend was taken a stage further in Shostakovich's next major chamber work, the Piano Quintet, written in 1940. Here the textures are crystal clear, recalling the restraint of the Twenty-Four Preludes, and looking forward to the later Preludes and Fugues. The piano writing is confined to simple, clearly-spaced parts—seldom more than two parts together in the first movement, unless a triadic accompaniment has to be accommodated. In the latter part of this movement Shostakovich uses one of his characteristic chamber-music devices: partial canonic entries are handed from piano to strings in an easy dialogue. The following fugue takes its place as one of the most balanced and expressive in the whole of the composer's output (Ex. 14). Taking as its obvious model the fugue which opens Beethoven's String Quartet Op. 131, it works its way

through a series of strict entries, integrating the various episodes into the texture with notable success. The Scherzo is again well planned, with a good deal of dry wit concealed within its apparently stiff contrapuntal progress. In contrast, the Intermezzo starts as a simple dialogue between a cantilena violin line and a walking pizzicato cello part, with later support from repeated piano triads. The atmosphere generated is one of serenity, an impression reinforced by the almost exclusively diatonic harmonies. The last movement admits some elements of the required cheerful resolution but is still sufficiently restrained and private in style to bring it into close alignment with the rest of the work. Its pace is slower than the normal Shostakovich finale, and the elliptical humour peeps out from a predominantly serious texture. A significant fact about this movement is that the shape is quite recognizably that of sonata form, with a first subject in G and the second, more concise subject in D. And, again as if to make quite clear to the listener that this is a work of consciously limited scale, the movement narrows down to a simple restatement of its main material, ending quietly, with a complete absence of histrionics.

The dichotomy between Shostakovich's private and public worlds could not be more clearly shown than by the contrast between the Piano Quintet and the work which appeared just over one year later—the Seventh Symphony. It was written during the siege of Leningrad (1941), and was conceived as 'an image of the war'. But from an artistic point of view, it represents a return to the monolithic world of the Fourth Symphony, with all that this implies in terms of duration (fifty-five minutes in this case) and orchestration. In addition to the large standard orchestra—once more using two harps—Shostakovich calls for an extra group of ten brass instruments. The symphony can only be viewed in relation to its programme. It is, in effect, a gigantic symphonic poem, and the various contrasts lose their impact and meaning if they are taken out of their particular wartime context. Stripped of their programmatic foundation, the symphony's huge gestures seem hollow: their kernel of musical thought is so much smaller than their surface area would suggest. And it is this distortion of image, rather than the local background, which has caused the work to slide into limbo fairly quickly.

Understandably, the following two years were not prolific. Not only was this the grimmest period of the war, but the composer was also engaged on an enterprise which was abortive—his opera *The Gamblers*. In 1943, Shostakovich produced his Second Piano Sonata, Op. 64. As in a number of earlier keyboard pieces, he uses a pattern of continuous figuration set against fairly simple themes (Ex. 15). In essence, the

Ex. 15

work is accessible to the performer of average ability; unlike the First Sonata, it does not require a virtuoso to steer a path through great technical difficulties. Two-part writing carries the argument, and the march-like second subject confines itself entirely to a simple triadic accompaniment. More important, the formal plan does not venture outside a straight-forward juxtaposition of these two themes; there is little that can be described as development, for Shostakovich, here as in an increasing number of works, relies on the quality of his themes, rather than their treatment, to carry the listener through the areas of statement and counter-statement that comprise the movement. This ground-plan, symbolizing per-haps the conflict-free dialogue of socialist realism (sic!) has appealed to the composer on a number of occasions, even where the style is nominally symphonic. Its lack of introspective con-volution neatly avoids the dreaded charge of formalism. Un-fortunately for the Soviet critics, the middle movement is much more enigmatic. Harmonically, it is remarkably enterprising for its context, for in spite of a recurrent emphasis on the A♭ tonality from which it takes its starting point, there is a notice-able freedom of manoeuvre, an extension of thought which the composer no doubt justified by the slowness of pace. Needless to say, a number of Soviet critics seized on this movement as a reversion to the bad old days of self-indulgent chromaticism. Between the sonata and the next chamber work, the Second String Quartet, Shostakovich produced his Eighth Symphony (1943). Again it 'recreated the impact of war on the Russians', as well as containing specific references to the Fifth Symphony. There are distinct signs that chamber music was still very much on the composer's mind however, for the last movement's orchestration is notably more re-strained and the mood more questioning than in the normal finale.

The Second String Quartet (1944) was a great advance on the previous chamber works, not so much from the point of view of its range of expression but in terms of technical freedom and mastery. It shows these qualities in four inter-related ways. First, particularly in the opening movement, the basic ideas are short motifs which govern the progress of the musical thought almost exclusively. The three motifs (marked *a*, *b*, *c*) in this first movement, for instance, are all contained within the initial theme (Ex. 16), and the rest of the movement

Ex. 16

—including the apparently forceful second subject—is entirely derived from these elements. Because of the emphasis on motivic development, Shostakovich can allow himself more metrical and rhythmic freedom than ever before. This second facet of advance shows itself not only in the displaced rhythms of the opening movement but in the across-the-bar phrasing of the inner movements. Thus the third movement (Valse), though starting out in simple triple time can accommodate changes to 4/4 and even 5/4 time in the course of its easy flow. The third advance, again related, is in the mixture of monodic and contrapuntal textures. At times Shostakovich pits his motifs against one another, or uses a single motif in close imitation or canon—an essentially neo-classical device. At other times he extends a motif horizontally, producing a melody with triadic accompaniment. Both these devices had been used frequently in previous works, but they had never been employed in such free or close combination. The remaining area of advance is harmonic, with all that this implies in terms of an expansion of tonality and the incorporation of passing dissonances. Very often, the latter occur because slightly differing versions of the same motif appear simultaneously; or a very close passage of imitation may contain entries in which odd accidentals differ from the original. In either case, the result is a clash which adds spice without fundamentally disturbing the harmonic flow. From a tonal point of view, the fact that the whole structure gains its meaning from the interplay of easily recognizable motifs means that less burden is placed on tonality; the more well defined the motivic texture, the more ambiguous the tonality can afford to be.

In the Second String Quartet, Shostakovich found for himself the language which served as the basis for all his subsequent chamber works, and, with modification, for some of the string concertos as well. Characteristically, he did not immediately press ahead from this vantage point. Instead, he turned outwards once again, completing the Ninth Symphony which had in fact been lying in the background during the composition of the Second String Quartet. Shostakovich's first plan for the symphony had been to include solo singers and chorus, but he drew back from this because of the fear of 'drawing immodest analogies'—an obvious reference to Beethoven's Ninth. When the symphony finally appeared in 1945, it was clear that Shostakovich had abandoned the original monumental programme—'the awakening of the millions'. In its place appeared a small-scale sinfonietta-like piece, without any explicit programme but with a good deal of wit and joie-de-vivre in its compact pages.

The only subsequent work to see the light of day before Zhdanov's 1948 outburst was the Third String Quartet (1946). It takes the composer's thought a step further by introducing thematic cross-references from one movement to another, while reverting in character to the direct statement approach of the First Quartet. Thus in the first movement the two main themes alternate, play against each other, and combine in odd proportions, to produce an effect that is more unified than might appear at first glance. Shostakovich concentrates on the horizontal connections between his themes and tends to ignore the possibilities for contrast that they may possess. In the second movement he almost manages to include a twelve-note theme (allowing for the repetitions that are necessary for his metrical scheme), though there is no attempt to follow up this phenomenon. But it is in the next movement that the composer produces some of his most characteristic music. Its restless energy is reinforced by an interesting basic irregularity of pulse (Ex. 17), sustained throughout the movement. And its

Ex. 17

urgency, later to be recalled in the scherzos of the Tenth and Eleventh symphonies, continues unabated to the final bar. During the same period, Shostakovich also began work on his First Violin Concerto, but Zhdanov's attack delayed its appearance until the mid-fifties.

44

THE SECOND CRISIS

The storm which burst over the heads of a number of major musical figures at the notorious meetings early in 1948 had in fact been threatening to break since the end of the war, for a number of attempts had been made to impose Marxist orthodoxy as part of a gigantic propaganda campaign to help the country's recovery. Undoubtedly, the major composers were less than enthusiastically creative when it came to the celebration of the thirtieth anniversary of the Revolution. Shostakovich, it was true, was busy on his cantata *Poem of the Fatherland*, but as we have seen his symphonic style had veered sharply away from the massive or the celebratory. Prokofiev was writing his Sixth Symphony; Miaskovsky was apparently busy on nothing at all. Obviously the composers were collectively lacking in fervour, and the stage was set for an onslaught of epic proportions. The immediate target used by Zhdanov was the première of a weak piece by Muradeli, an opera called *The Great Fellowship*. But at the three meetings of the Composers' Union this mediocre work was soon forgotten. The real targets—the major figures—found themselves under a barrage of ponderous rhetoric; they were deviationist, occupied by private whims, pathologically discordant, and so on.

Shostakovich made two speeches at this time, not as abject as some observers have indicated, but clearly bewildered at the force of the accusations. For a time, the effect was serious: it widened once more the gap between private and public utterance, and led to the temporary suppression of the First Violin Concerto, a fine work. In the next eighteen months Shostakovich completed his Jewish Folk Poems, Op. 79 and another diffuse cantata, *Song of the Woods*, but it is significant that he waited until the death of Stalin in 1953 before releasing his Tenth Symphony. Towards the end of 1949, however, he did manage to write his Fourth String Quartet. There is every sign in this work of a gradual strengthening of resolve, a growing determination to return to the path from which he had been so violently diverted. During the two opening movements of this quartet, the form is somewhat unconvincing because of the rambling nature of the thematic material. But by the third movement, the writing is more characteristic, and the last movement is unusual in its sequence of ideas, and enterprising in its treatment of them. Understandably, however, the quartet as a whole is not one of the outstanding works of the series; it is a reaffirmation of the genre, rather than an exploration of new thought.

In a way, the next major work was also retrospective; it drew the strands of earlier works together, and consolidated them in a set of pieces which occupy a most important place in Shostakovich's output: the Twenty-Four Preludes and Fugues for Piano, written in 1951. The immediate inspiration for the work was his visit to Leipzig for the two-hundredth anniversary of the death of Bach, whose influence is apparent throughout. Shostakovich's first plan was to write a series of polyphonic exercises to perfect his own skill, but this plan broadened to produce a free-ranging yet carefully controlled kaleidoscope of musical sound. Many types of piece merge in this work—classical sarabande (Prelude 1), figured chorale (Prelude 4), pianistic étude (Preludes 2 and 21), and passacaglia (Prelude 12). Perhaps the most characteristic of the preludes, however, are those which take their inspiration from Russian national sources—the unison chorus effects of Prelude 3, the marching-song background to Prelude 9, or the traditional flavour of Preludes 16 and 20. The success with which Shostakovich welds together this multifarious assembly of musical

46

types is remarkable. The fugues, though more strictly governed and limited by their form, also reveal a variety of mood and style. From two voices (Fugue 9) to five (Fugue 13), their layout is differentiated, and the diatonicism of a fugue such as No. 1 is contrasted with the eleven-note chromaticism of No. 15, just as the melodic range of a diminished fifth in Fugue 19 is contrasted with the wider range of melody in a fugue such as No. 12. Throughout, the relationship of a prelude to its fugue varies. Some lead on naturally, as in No. 1, others present a sharp opposition (No. 3). The final fugue is in some ways an exception to the group. Consisting of a long crescendo, it develops into a mixture between concert-étude and sonata-like structure, and could easily be detached to form a separate entity. And yet even this one does not break out of the general style of the whole work. On the contrary, it is its culmination, epitomizing the range of piano writing contained in the cycle. Apart from all internal considerations, the Preludes and Fugues are of crucial importance in Shostakovich's career; they are a statement of his personal convictions about musical style, and a re-affirmation, after a period of intense difficulties, of the keyboard from which his art has always stemmed.

Also begun in 1951, the Fifth String Quartet shows the influence of this piano work very clearly in its use of polyphony and the thematic integration which permeates its related movements. As can be seen (Ex. 18), the opening consists of a

Ex. 18

number of suspended fragments, using incidentally the minor-major third constellation which was fast becoming one of Shostakovich's particular obsessions. The music returns to the viola's fixed point constantly, and the whole piece moves outward from this starting point. Themes are elongated, driven upward to the inevitable climactic centre, and repeated over an ambivalent rhythmic pattern. With one held note, a high F, supported by chords, one of the composer's most brilliant chamber movements joins on to an easier Andante, though this again is a movement where the quality of invention is high. The movement is, in fact, a hint of the shape which, two years later, Shostakovich was to use for the opening of his Tenth Symphony.

This symphony dates from the year of Stalin's death, and perhaps owes some of its outstanding qualities to the anticipation of a more liberal musical atmosphere in Russia. Its first movement is Shostakovich's best symphonic piece; it has a heroic, epic stature—a huge edifice raising itself stage by stage from a markedly restrained opening, through an increasingly impassioned development and central climax, to a final return to the point from which it started out. The main material of the movement, with its three separate strands, each capable of extension, (Ex. 19, a, b, c,) is extremely simple. And in fact Shostakovich greatly increases the range and time-scale on which his themes operate by extending and developing each

Ex. 19

in turn before the appearance of any formal 'development section'. As the movement progresses, it becomes obvious that the leisurely way in which the ideas are presented sets the proportions for the whole in a manner that would not have been possible with any strict conformity to sonata form. In the discussions which the Union of Soviet Composers organized after the first performance, Shostakovich repeated his self-criticism that this opening movement did not succeed in becoming what he had dreamed of for a long time, namely a 'real symphonic allegro'. From the nature of the material, this was of course impossible; the themes are similar in mood and lyrical in their continuity, and therefore do not present the formal contrasts necessary for a sonata allegro form. But together, these themes coalesce into one of the most extended arch-structures in symphonic music. In fact, the piece, apparently written at white heat, is utterly consistent in aim. It is the lyricist's perfect answer to the problem of extended form—a combination of slow movement, cumulative extension, and varied recapitulation, without strain and without any of the awkward transitions that had afflicted some of Shostakovich's earlier attempts in the same style.

The scherzo, short by comparison, stems from a restless, climbing motif, and expands to a noisy, bustling set of tutti statements in which the solid brass chords, offset by high strings and screaming woodwind figuration, are the important elements. The scoring remains fairly heavy, and the percussion plays an increasingly noticeable role in defining the pulse of the movement, until, with a sudden upward chromatic flourish, the piece ends as abruptly as it began. Virtually everything stems from the first few bars; the opposing motif is still a clear derivative from this single source. It confirms again that the best of this composer's works subsist on monothematic foundations, and that continuous development widening out from this centre and finally returning to it is his most natural formal plan. The third movement, a compromise between dance and song form, points to this fact once more. Although the main theme contains two elements, there is no attempt to introduce an opposing theme; the whole movement grows from this twin stem. The second element, by the way, is of interest in that it contains the composer's own motto—DSCH —as its anchor point; something which recurs with such concentrated fury in his Eighth String Quartet. And the ambiguity of major-minor thirds which is at the root of this phrase, has of course, been the main harmonic and melodic source for the whole of the first movement, as well as for much of the scherzo.

LATER WORKS

As already mentioned, the First Violin Concerto was written early in 1948; it was originally given the opus number 77, but it had to wait eight years before it finally appeared, with the revised opus number 99. The work is dedicated to David Oistrakh, and there are many signs that the soloist played an active part in the preparation of the score, helping to clarify the varied requirements of string range and tone. The concerto has a number of unconventional elements; it is a virtuoso concerto, but not consistently so; there are technical difficulties in abundance, but the thematic content of the work does not allow these to play a significant role; the solo part is integrated with the orchestral texture in a way that is not characteristic of the romantic 'competitive' concerto. As a result of this attitude, the first movement ignores the conventions of sonata form, and becomes a contemplative, virtually mono-thematic nocturne. Its static chords and repetitive melodic line may act as an extended introduction to the subsequent scherzo, but it is a far cry from the usual concerto first movement. The solo part, while leading the orchestra, produces no tension, and there are no histrionics from either soloist or orchestra. The scherzo's main theme sounds like a speeded-up trial run for the third movement of the Tenth Symphony, but instead of the symphony's mixture of formal dance and extended melody the effect here is one of bustle and provocative noise. A fleeting tapestry of sound hurries past, hardly pausing to alight on any one theme or phrase. The analogy with the Tenth Symphony continues into the finale of the concerto, for the similarity of the theme and its accompaniment to the main Allegro of the symphony's last movement is striking.

In his next work, the Sixth String Quartet, (1956), Shosta-kovich relaxed his grip on both form and texture—a contrast with the Fifth Quartet. The structure is much more simple, and the first movement has an easy Mahlerian lilt, and more than a hint of the dance about it. The idiom is predominantly diatonic, as is that of the second movement. Only with the third do we find a return to the atmosphere of the Fifth Quar-tet. This is a freely-worked passacaglia—a favourite third-movement form in the later quartets; simple in shape, but eloquent.

The huge Eleventh Symphony (1957) represents a return to the world of the large-scale programme symphony—it is sub-titled '1905', and depicts the abortive revolution of that year. It concentrates its energies into a furiously combative second movement, a piece remarkable for its sustained, enormous span. But much more important from a purely musical point of view is the First Cello Concerto (1959), Shostakovich's finest concerto as far as musical content is concerned. From the very outset it has an inexorable drive and concentration. For once, there are hardly any episodes or obvious transitions; the argument is sustained without interruption or dilution, and the end of the first movement is as sudden as it is inevitable. The solo part carries much of the musical burden, and it ex-plores an enormous pitch range—a mark of the composer's confidence in the soloist, Rostropovich, for whom the work was written. The first movement is unusual for the fact that its basic tempo is considerably faster than most of Shostakovich's opening sections. In fact, although it contains very little con-trasting material, this movement fulfils the composer's dream of a true symphonic allegro. As a result of the strength of this opening, he can afford to relax in the quiet, meditative second movement. Its roots stretch back into folk-song, and the rich lyrical possibilities of the solo instrument are fully exploited. The contrast with the first movement goes much further than

52

the difference in tempo: one might say that the metabolic rate of the movement is also lowered, since the rate at which the musical material is introduced is less urgent and its treatment less insistent. The third section is a connecting episode between this meditative piece and the finale. It takes the form of a cadenza for the soloist, becoming progressively more complex in its declamation, until it breaks into the boisterous last movement. Like so many energetic and 'optimistic' finales, this one is less than perfect musically; as so often, there seems a gap between the pace of the movement and its real content. But it is still superior to most of the other examples of this type.

After the Cello Concerto came two quartets in quick succession. The Seventh Quartet (1960) begins with two sections which are relatively unexceptional; development is of little importance here, though Shostakovich does make varied use of his opening phrases. But the finale is much more enterprising. An interesting point is that both the first and last movements are divided into two halves, duple and triple. Where the first movement's motif has a falling line, the finale's rises, but the switch to triple time half way through is the same in both movements. Another factor shared by these outer movements is their fluency of line, taking in its stride the various rhythmic irregularities that are used.

The Eighth Quartet, also written in 1960, is a special case which deserves a closer look. It could almost be described as an autobiography in music, since there are many references to previous works, and many statements of the composer's own motto: D, E♭, C, B, or DSCH. The work was inspired by a visit to the war-scarred city of Dresden, and its prevailing mood of seriousness is overtly programmatic. But beyond this programme it carries, in a different way from any of the other quartets, a feeling of anguish, the haunting pain of personal mortality. One of Shostakovich's increasingly recurrent obsessions had been to base a motif on the interval of a minor third, then to expand this interval by a semitone to produce a hint of a brighter sound, only to withdraw to the original minor again. The Tenth Symphony, for example, gains its entire harmonic and melodic atmosphere from this procedure. It is significant that this device is embedded in the DSCH motif. The quartet begins with a series of canonic entries on this motif (Ex. 20). A deliberate feeling of tonal ambiguity is built up, since the cello, viola, and first violin entries encompass all twelve semitones of

Ex. 20

the octave, with D♭ delayed until the cello's sixth complete bar. There is something of a harmonic impasse around bars 9 and 10, as Shostakovich attempts to provide a triadic resolution to his polyphonic texture, but the ambiguity remains, with a unison assertion of DSCH again. On the last note of the phrase the harmony shifts briefly to E minor-major, but as the final note B (first violin) becomes the starting-point for a quotation from the opening of the First Symphony, the harmonic basis moves back quickly to C minor, the home key. The rest of the movement, including a quotation from the development theme of the Fifth Symphony's first movement, remains very firmly anchored around C, allowing for the expected major-minor syndrome, and also a few bars' excursion to A minor. The whole pattern—chromatic opening, subsequent stabilization by triadic harmonies, and closing restatement (this time more chordal) shows every aspect of Shostakovich's mature style. The underlying tonality is never lost sight of, though the composer allows himself much freedom in the way of incidental dissonances or extended false relations. In particular, the interchangeability of major and minor thirds over the same root has by now become a permanent feature of the landscape. And from the point of view of the easy co-existence of contrapuntal and harmonic language, the work is outstanding. Both the second and third movements rely heavily on the DSCH motif, and the third also contains an explicit reference to the First Cello Concerto, a quotation which grows into an extended cello theme linking the third to the fourth movement, where it becomes the main source for the theme. The final movement mirrors the first, except for the fact that it has only the smallest hint of the First Symphony.

The pendulum swing of Shostakovich's output, from complex to simple, gargantuan to economical, programmatic to abstract, has been a consistent phenomenon. After the rigours of the Eighth Quartet, it is little surprise to find that the next work is not only big, but also diffuse. Dedicated to Lenin, and called the '1917 Symphony', the Twelfth Symphony is not particularly noteworthy. There are few points of interest, apart from the irregular vitality of the third movement. But the Thirteenth Symphony, written in 1962, is a very different matter. A setting of five poems by Yevtushenko, it is a symphony in which a deep personal involvement and protest can be felt. Yevtushenko had already collided with the authorities because of the first of these poems, 'Babi Yar'. It was obvious, then, that Shostakovich was inviting similar disapproval by setting this poem as it stood. The content of the poem is indeed sombre. Its subject is the place, Babi Yar, where Jews were massacred by the Germans during the war. Without doubt, the section which aroused the fury of the authorities was the one in which Yevtushenko reminds his audience that there are also anti-semitic trends in Russia. After the first performance on 18 December 1962, Yevtushenko did add some lines to indicate that it was not only Jews who died at Babi Yar. But the symphony has still had a very chequered career in Russia. The musical content is sparse, severe, pared down to the bones of line and accompaniment. There is no section that could be called a real Allegro in either tempo or mood, in spite of the presence of at least two poems that might have called for lighter treatment. The part for solo bass adopts a declamatory, sometimes hortatory tone from the beginning, and much of the chorus part is confined to long held notes and chords. The orchestration is, for a Shostakovich symphony, remarkably restrained, and the climaxes are short-lived. And nowhere in the whole of Shostakovich's output is the influence of Mussorgsky so apparent.

After this symphony, Shostakovich returned once more to the haven of the string quartet, adding three more to his list during the next three years (1964–6). The Ninth Quartet makes no attempt to explore the same depths as No. 8. On the contrary, the lines are broader, more lyrical, and the fierce use of canonic imitation has virtually disappeared. Within the five linked movements there is a fairly wide range of mood, from a highly expressive adagio to the mordant wit of the finale. In spite of the work's lack of polyphonic texture when compared with some of the earlier quartets, it does continue their habit of carrying related themes and phrases over from one movement to another. And the final coda emphasizes the similarity that has existed between the various themes. The Tenth Quartet dates from the same year. The ground plan of its opening movement follows the chromatic-triadic polarity of the Eighth Quartet, but without that work's economy. Its calmer sense of balance does, however, create an extended ana-crusis for the fast and furious second movement, which seems at first glance to be parodying the same theme from the development of the first movement of the Fifth Symphony. But, at this stage the basic material of Shostakovich's melodic lines is so similar in essence, especially in the quicker movements, that it is no longer useful to point out sources for the themes; they share a common outline and a common repertoire of intervallic devices. As far as thematic integration between the movements goes, the Tenth Quartet is as characteristic as any. The theme of the passacaglia, for instance, recurs in the last movement, where it acts as a slower counterpart to that movement's own more fleeting material; and at the very end of the work, much of the previous music is recapitulated.

String Quartet No. 11 dates from 1966 and is written, rather curiously, in the form of a suite of seven interlinked movements. All seven take as their foundation one of two motifs— the theme of the introduction, or the theme of the following scherzo. By linking all the movements Shostakovich goes some way towards unifying the whole work, though it must be admitted that the fleeting interchange of mood and tempo still produces a more fragmentary effect than in the previous quartets. The writing here is almost exclusively of the melody-and-accompaniment type, and a good deal of it is limited to two real parts.

This work was followed by two more string concertos, for cello and violin respectively, neither of which attains the level of Shostakovich's earlier example in the same genre. The Second Cello Concerto is a very insubstantial work, in spite of a length well over thirty minutes. Its themes lack the conviction and drive of the First Cello Concerto, and the overall atmosphere suggests a composer working against the grain of his own needs. The writing for the soloist is assured, similar prominence is given again to the horns, and the relation between soloist and orchestra is perhaps even better calculated than in the earlier work. But next to that, this is a poor shadow diminished in vitality, its concentration dissipated. More interesting is the Second Violin Concerto, which again contains points of contact with its companion concerto for violin, but is actually closer in spirit to the First Cello Concerto. Here, the division of the work into three movements allows the finale to incorporate some of the qualities of a scherzo—a mood much more suited to Shostakovich—and for this reason the ending does not seem so insubstantial. Another welcome change is that although the first movement conforms to the arch shape with central climax which seems mandatory for this composer's style, it does not in this case have the usual cyclical tendency; it does not return to its point of germination. When it comes to the actual content of the themes, we find Shostakovich's primary obsessions strongly in evidence. The very first theme is a variant (transposed) of the DSCH motto, and this forms the main melodic material for the whole movement. Once this opening phrase has been presented, it is subjected to a treatment parallel to that in the opening of the First Cello Concerto. The pressure slowly builds up around the soloist, the pitch range of the dialogue widens until the familiar situation of orchestral extremes—top woodwind facing the lower strings, or horns facing upper strings—is played out against various solo figurations. The soloist, in fact, holds the balance between these extremes. Shostakovich leaves out trumpets and trombones, and although this makes the balance easier, it does increase the significance of the role played by the horns, particularly the first horn. The second movement is deceptive. At first, it seems as if it might turn out to be a simple folk-derived piece; but in reality it is much more carefully wrought than its early bars would suggest. Its clarity of texture brings it into close alignment with the composer's chamber-music style, and its chromaticism is noticeably more free than in most of the previous public works. Towards the end of the movement, for instance, Shostakovich seems about to launch himself into total chromaticism, leaving behind any underpinning tonality (Ex. 21). As the passage resolves itself, the listener realizes that he has been allowed to savour not a

Ex. 21

main idea, but only a bridge passage of unusual enterprise. When it comes to the last movement, the most interesting section is undoubtedly the cadenza, since it is both a virtuoso vehicle and a survey of the thematic content of the work as a whole. But from then on, the 'public' Shostakovich of the earlier symphonies takes over. He whips up surplus energy with the expertise of a ringmaster. Musical interest is minimal, but the purpose, as always in these finales, is as old as theatre itself.

In two of his latest works, the Twelfth String Quartet and the Fourteenth Symphony, Shostakovich returns to the predominant instrumental forms in his output. To take the larger work first, the Fourteenth Symphony, like its predecessor, consists of a series of vocal settings. But whereas the earlier work used poems exclusively by Yevtushenko, this one takes poems by writers as disparate as Apollinaire, Lorca, and Rilke. The theme which unifies them is the image of death, haunting even the few musical settings which could conceivably have been more lighthearted. This is Shostakovich at his most sombre—a prolonged and intense meditation on personal mortality, with few opportunities for relief or contrast. The scoring is scaled down to chamber dimensions: two singers— soprano and bass—with an orchestra of nineteen strings and percussion, including such tuned instruments as bells, vibraphone and xylophone, and the celesta as a delicate extra. The eleven short movements make up an overall shape which, in outline at least, is the kind which Shostakovich would produce for a purely instrumental symphony. Thus, the first poem, Lorca's 'De Profundis', serves as the basis for one of the composer's usual slow symphonic introductions. The strings meditate around the poem, very much in the style of the opening movement of the Eleventh Symphony, or the introduction to the First Violin Concerto—a static, sad, and rather brooding adagio, its tonality diffused, its predominantly minor intervals coming in for extensive quotation later on in the work. In the short second movement, the poem, again by Lorca, talks of death haunting the tavern, mingling with the sound of the guitar, and the smell of salt and warm blood. This macabre piece gives rise to a busy allegretto which combines the functions of a symphonic scherzo with the urgency of one of the composer's development sections. The strings scurry about in familiar manner, or imitate the rhythm of the guitar with sardonic emphasis. The lines of the poem are distributed fairly evenly amid this welter of string sound, as if to make quite clear that they are merely the props supporting Shostakovich's thought. With hardly a break, the third poem, Apollinaire's 'Lorelei', follows. Throughout this setting, the composer uses a remarkably free juxtaposition of semitonal dissonances, with sudden reversions to naive unisons—a contrast which never fails to produce the effect of deliberate crudity.

The rest of the work is less symphonic in layout, relying instead on the contrasts of mood between adjacent poems. For the tenth setting—Rilke's 'Death of the Poet'—Shostakovich repeats some of the material from the opening of the symphony; and, to reinforce the fact that all the poems have, in their various ways, centred on images of death, the final poem, again by Rilke, points out the constant pervasiveness of death, 'even in the hour of highest happiness'. The repeated chord which ends the work (Ex. 22) shows how far Shostakovich has

Ex. 22

travelled from the major chords and triadic optimism with which all his middle-period symphonies were obliged to end.

In the very recent Fifteenth Symphony, a purely orchestral work, Shostakovich returns to his quest for 'a true symphonic allegro'. He goes right through the fairly long first movement without a single change of speed. The initial motif recalls the First Cello Concerto in its brevity and drive. But before long, an even more pervasive phrase comes into view—the Allegro Vivace theme from Rossini's *William Tell* Overture. With its unflagging mobility, it acts as a rallying point for all the related phrases throughout the movement. The rest of the symphony also has its quota of outside references. In the Adagio, there is a direct quotation from his own Eleventh Symphony, and the Scherzo makes use of his DSCH motif. The Finale is headed by a quotation—the Fate motif from Wagner's *Ring*—and, like a sombre warning, this recurs twice later on. Shostakovich points to a more personal significance by allowing the brass to modify it in order to show its relationship to the DSCH motif. The mask of apparent easy activity earlier in the symphony makes way for the fundamental pessimism and complexity of his own temperament.

LANGUAGE OF THE TWELFTH QUARTET

Although written before the Fourteenth Symphony, the Twelfth Quartet has been left to the end because, to date, it presents in the most succinct form a summary of Shostakovich's harmonic and melodic language, as developed in the chamber works. A quotation from the opening bars (Ex. 23) will show a number of his mature characteristics. The total chromaticism of the first bar, for instance, is a means of postponing the direct tonal statement which follows. Although twelve semitones are incorporated in this initial gambit, their

Ex. 23

use is in no way parallel to serialism. But their presence is nevertheless indicative of a general widening of vocabulary, a motivic poise and sophistication which would have been inconceivable in the works written ten years earlier. These two opening bars present the diametrically opposed areas of composition in Shostakovich's output. On the one hand, his maturity and mastery are bent on expanding beyond the confines of the triad. But his innate conservatism ensures that the last quaver of this enterprising first bar is the traditional dominant for the tonic which follows. He has held back the tonal resolution for the space of a full bar at fairly slow tempo, but beyond that point he is not prepared to go. Characteristically, his statement of the home key is without ambiguity; indeed, the next three bars are stable to a degree recalling the accompaniment to a number of his very early symphonic themes; the metabolic rate of the music appears to slow down, making the first bar seem eccentric in the new context. But

66

this is an illusion. Having balanced the two aspects of his musical thought—incidentally, in proportions that would be unthinkable for a radical Western composer—Shostakovich goes on to explore, very gradually, the main elements—the minor second, and the fourth—of his opening bar. Thus, his main idea concentrates around the minor second, emphasizing its effect by placing it in false relation to the accompaniment. Throughout this passage Shostakovich preserves a continuous flow; every event is placed in a horizontal context, presenting a tapestry of seamless thought rather than a set of strongly contrasted ideas. This horizontal 'spread' is responsible for the dilution of harmonic incident, and it is a full twenty more bars before the two main intervals of the movement have been thoroughly digested. And it is noticeable that the tonic is constantly reiterated, usually by the cello. At a crucial point, the link to the second subject—bar 29—encapsulates both the chromaticism of the opening and the false relation present in the main idea.

The change to triple time at this point is reminiscent of the First Symphony's opening movement, though a comparison will show the vastly more sophisticated and flexible method used here. In place of the earlier work's obvious signalling of the new theme, the quartet's second subject emerges smoothly, and goes on immediately to develop the tension-resolution syndrome of the opening; all twelve semitones are spread through the four bars given to the first violin, and a similar harmonic stasis follows during the next four bars. With one exception—a tiny motif of four repeated quavers—the entire material of the movement has now been stated. From these basic motifs, Shostakovich weaves a continuous discourse, an essentially linear surface, through which the general shape of sonata form is discernible, but which does not rely on sonata-confrontations for its intrinsic existence. There is a clear development section, though under these conditions, it is of

67

limited range, preferring to amalgamate and fuse together the basic strands, as a short example will show (Ex. 24). At the end of the movement, Shostakovich anticipates his final cadence, holding a pedal D♭ on the cello before the closing statement—a characteristic device when the atmosphere is more that of an extended prelude than that of sonata form. One further point; as in so many of Shostakovich's works, the almost casual juxtaposition of chromatic and diatonic language

Ex. 24

is more disconcerting within a continuous, discreet texture than it would be within a more consciously 'primitive' setting. The swing from dissonance to consonance, or for that matter from dense texture to simple unison, makes a greater impact because it occurs without apparent calculation.

The remaining movement of the quartet is much more substantial, complex and interesting, combining as it does the functions of scherzo, sonata-development, and general recapitulation for the whole work. In the shape of an enormous inverted arch, it nevertheless gains most of its impetus from a very

small motif—the semiquaver figure stated by the cello at the
outset (Ex. 25). This motif dominates every manoeuvre in the

Ex. 25

main outer sections—the scherzo material—and shows a close
relationship to the first movement material recapitulated towards the end of the middle section. Too much can be made
of the fact that the opening bars contain all twelve semitones,
since the important thing here is their support of the main

motif. They are not used in rotation; they do not form a single pervasive entity on which, *as a totally recurring unit*, the rest of the movement is based. Indeed, the one feature they share with other chromatic statements in the movement is the mere fact that within their scope, all possible semitones have been incorporated. The order, the position in the sequence of notes varies freely. And the reason for this is simple: Shostakovich is much more interested in the motivic possibilities of his material—particularly from a rhythmic point of view—than he is in ordering that material by interval-logic. The principle of rotation does not of itself concern him. This explains the fact that almost unlimited 'twelve-note rows' can be uncovered in the course of the movement, without any one of them dominating the melodic potentialities. All the same, Shostakovich has never before allowed his basic ideas to rely so exclusively on total chromaticism: there are areas in this piece which leave tonality far behind, as they insist on the right of the major seventh or minor ninth to dictate the entire vertical logic of a musical passage. The technique is closely related to the insistent, reiterative use of a small motif in many of the earlier works—the First Cello Concerto and many of the symphonic scherzi spring immediately to mind—and it is this motivic bias which allows Shostakovich to commit the ultimate sin, from a serialist's point of view. In recapitulating his scherzo, he reformulates the main motif to produce a straightforward, crudely tonal statement. For the composer, it is sufficiently 'positive', as well as being close to the original utterance, to form the resolution of the tense opening bars. To make sure that its ultimate stability is not lost on his audience, he repeats this cadential material with the subtlety of a sledge-hammer (Ex. 26). There is no serial illogicality here. Shostakovich is interested in his motifs mainly as linear thematic devices: they are used for their own sake, not as the mere audible symbols of a superior, all-pervasive abstraction. They

Ex. 26

impinge, and are remembered, more for their metrical or rhythmic grouping than for their intervallic order. Many of the casual dissonances scattered throughout the movement also owe their existence more to the incidental clash of lines than to vertical tension or intervallic succession. Example 27 shows the typical result when two, and later three, lines meet in combination. The horizontal impetus produces not only the

Ex. 27

semitonal bottleneck at the middle of the fourth bar, but also the unconcerned doubling of the F sharp at the beginning of the second bar. For the linear-minded, unison and dissonance are not necessarily so widely separated. And this, apart from any ideological considerations, explains why Shostakovich can reverse the usual order of things: his climactic bars can subsist on consonances, instead of the expected maximum concentration of dissonance.

But the ideological background is still important. Shostakovich obviously regards chromaticism as dangerous—the technical temptation of the devil—and will go to great lengths, first to justify its existence or place it in context, and second to resolve the problems it poses before the end of the work. Not even the pessimistic, enclosed Eighth Quartet can leave its ambiguous chromaticisms unresolved; it finishes on a comparatively open C minor chord. And the present quartet does not break this pattern. It has stretched tonality to breaking point and provided the clearest example of the composer straining at the gates of total chromaticism. But his conservatism reasserts itself in the end. For every chromatic statement of the basic motifs, there is a counterbalancing tonal statement. The tension between the two is a major part of the fundamental impact of the music. The opposed polarities revitalize one another—the tonality is expanded, the chromaticism constantly underpinned. And however much the note values and constituent intervals may vary in the course of the movement, Shostakovich is able to pursue a single goal—to create a discourse of symphonic proportions from tiny source-motifs.

STYLE AND INFLUENCE

The Twelfth Quartet provides a neat summary of Shostakovich's style and vocabulary. But, as pointed out in the introduction, the tension of polarities it reveals is not confined to any single work; it spreads right through the composer's output. And the swing of the pendulum could quite easily result in a further period of purely tonal writing, without invalidating either the chromatically enterprising 'internal' works, or the more relaxed external occasional pieces already written. The whole output is, in a sense, one huge work, with tensions distributed backwards and forwards through the various categories of composition. It is an essentially uneven manner of production, especially if one looks at isolated works, but it possesses qualities which cause it to expand far beyond its apparent linguistic boundaries. Thus, Shostakovich builds his edifice on certain stabilizing foundations. For him, the primary intervals of the harmonic series—octave, fifth, fourth, and the major and minor thirds—are the 'white' intervals. Ideologically, they represent outward-turning health and optimism. The fact that they also form the basis of diatonic tonality ensures that whatever diversions may occur in the course of a movement, the work will always have its resolution in a tonal cadence derived from one or other of these constituents.

In the chamber works, his language has became increasingly concerned with the last two of these intervals—the major and minor third—presented over a fixed tonic. And this is the method by which ambiguity was introduced in the public works of the fifties. Over the static tonic a fleetingly interchangeable situation could occur, so that sometimes it was

impossible to say which species of triad—major or minor—
was taking precedence. But in all these works—the First
Violin Concerto, and the Tenth and Eleventh symphonies in
particular—the all-important root remained in evidence as
justification for the ambiguities or simultaneous contradictions of the upper parts.

With the Eighth Quartet, Shostakovich moved further
away from this well-rooted foundation. His own motto—
DSCH—produced ambiguity not only in its first two intervals,
but also in the remaining two. Out of a mere four notes, therefore, there was a choice of four separate tonal roots—a situation which could not fail to drive the composer further away
from tonality, especially when, as in this quartet, the motto
was employed mainly in contrapuntal imitation of itself. A
cluster of works from the Eighth Quartet onwards exploited
these oblique possibilities with increasing boldness and freedom, though at any moment, the composer could retreat into
easy diatonic harmonies again. It is significant that it was an
autobiographical fragment—an interior thought—which provided this break-through.

In the latest works, Shostakovich expands yet further his
progress up the harmonic series, so to speak. From the Ninth
Quartet, his preoccupations are more and more concerned
with the smaller intervals—the major and minor seconds and
their respective inversions. In the Eleventh and Twelfth
Quartets, he no longer finds it necessary to reiterate the more
basic intervals of the harmonic series throughout the musical
texture. But they are implied: there is no moment, even in the
extreme second movement of the Twelfth Quartet, at which a
fundamental tonality cannot be deduced from the apparently
free play of chromaticism. And this is the reason for the logic
in sound, as distinct from on paper, behind the casual juxtaposition of tonal and chromatic, consonant and dissonant features
in this mature work. Shostakovich has widened his language

to a point which accommodates most of the harmonic series, and which significantly still builds on its diatonic foundations. There is no break in style; there is no theoretical revolution to delight the hearts of radical listeners. The position taken up is closer in fact to Hindemith, with his chromatic extension of traditional methods, than it is to Schoenberg. And ultimately it offers more in the way of contact between composer and listener. On the one hand, its reassertion of the primary foundation—the hierarchy of the harmonic series—is almost unique in worthwhile contemporary music, allowing it to communicate with an unprejudiced audience more vividly and with more immediacy than is possible with an arbitrarily imposed musical alphabet. It brings extremely disparate musical elements into close relationship. And on the other hand, it preserves and revitalizes forms which most Western composers can no longer utilize, except as self-conscious anachronisms—the tonal sonata, the fugue, or the suite. These are aspects of composition which may well turn out to be of more lasting importance than we can at present discern. Certainly, the exclusive exploration of the upper partials of the harmonic series in contemporary music will be seen in retrospect as too limited, too self-enclosed to form the basis for communication between creator and recipient.

By a unique set of circumstances, Shostakovich was subjected to pressure which pulled in the opposite direction from that usually experienced by twentieth-century composers. And it is the greatest tribute to his genius, as well as to his courage, that he rose like a phoenix from the conflagration surrounding his middle years, to preserve the best of his early stylistic possibilities and impose on them a wider vision, more disciplined, and capable of more variation. With all its inevitable contradictions, the language which culminates in the Twelfth Quartet offers one of the possible lifelines to contemporary music—a basis for communication in which the individual can pursue his own subjective path—the upper partials of his music, if you like—and yet remain in touch with the root unisons and simple consonances of the ordinary listener. An unfashionable thesis, but one which is triumphantly vindicated in Shostakovich's latest works, and which, at the present time, it would be foolish to ignore.

LIST OF SHOSTAKOVICH'S PRINCIPAL WORKS IN CHRONOLOGICAL ORDER

Three Fantastic Dances for Piano, Opus 5 (1922)
First Symphony, Opus 10 (1926)
Prelude and Scherzo for String Octet, Opus 11 (1924)
Piano Sonata No. 1, Opus 12 (1926)
Ten Aphorisms for Piano, Opus 13 (1926)
Second Symphony ('October'), Opus 14 (1927)
The Nose opera to libretto by Y. Preis, Opus 15 (1929) (First performance 1930)
Third Symphony, Opus 20 (1931)
Six Romanzas to Poems by Japanese Poets, Opus 21 (1928–31)
The Golden Age—ballet in 3 Acts, Opus 22 (1929–30)
The Bolt—ballet in 3 Acts, Opus 27 (1930–1)
Lady Macbeth of Mtsensk (later renamed *Katerina Ismailova*)
—opera to libretto by Y. Preis, Opus 29 (1930–2). (First performance 1934)
Twenty-Four Preludes for Piano, Opus 34 (1932–3)
Concerto for Piano, Trumpet and Strings, Opus 35 (1933)
Sonata for Cello and Piano, Opus 40 (1934)
Fourth Symphony, Opus 43 (1935–6)
Four Romanzas to verses by Pushkin, Opus 46 (1936)
Fifth Symphony, Opus 47 (1937)
First String Quartet, Opus 49 (1938)
Sixth Symphony, Opus 54 (1939)
Piano Quintet, Opus 57 (1940)
Seventh Symphony, Opus 60 (1941)
Leningrad Suite for Chorus and Orchestra, Opus 61 (1942)

Six Romances to Poems by Burns, Shakespeare, and Walter Raleigh, Opus 62 (1942)

The Gamblers—opera on Gogol's Story, Opus 63 (unfinished) (1942)

Piano Sonata No. 2, Opus 64 (1943)

Eighth Symphony, Opus 65 (1942)

Piano Trio, Opus 67 (1944)

Second String Quartet, Opus 69 (1944)

Ninth Symphony, Opus 70 (1945)

Third String Quartet, Opus 73 (1946)

Poem of the Fatherland, Opus 74 (1947)

Fourth String Quartet, Opus 83 (1949)

Twenty-Four Preludes and Fugues for Piano, Opus 87 (1950–1)

Ten Poems by Revolutionary Poets, Opus 88 (1950)

Fifth String Quartet, Opus 92 (1952)

Tenth Symphony, Opus 93 (1953)

Festive Overture, Opus 96 (1954)

First Violin Concerto, Opus 99 (first listed as Opus 77) (1947–8)

Sixth String Quartet, Opus 101 (1956)

Second Piano Concerto, Opus 102 (1956–7)

Eleventh Symphony, Opus 103 (1957)

First Cello Concerto, Opus 107 (1959)

Seventh String Quartet, Opus 108 (1960)

Eighth String Quartet, Opus 110 (1960)

Twelfth Symphony, Opus 112 (1961)

Thirteenth Symphony, (1962)

Ninth String Quartet, Opus 117 (1964)

Tenth String Quartet, Opus 118 (1964)

Eleventh String Quartet, Opus 122 (1966)

Second Cello Concerto, Opus 126 (1967)

Second Violin Concerto, Opus 129 (1968)

Twelfth String Quartet, Opus 133 (1968)

Fourteenth Symphony, Opus 135 (1969)

Fifteenth Symphony, Opus 141 (1971)